香港國際詩歌之夜 *2011*
INTERNATIONAL POETRY NIGHTS IN HONG KONG

編輯 Editors

方梓勳 Gilbert C. F. Fong

陳嘉恩 Shelby K. Y. Chan

柯夏智 Lucas Klein

何潔賢 Amy Ho Kit Yin

北島 Bei Dao

陳克華

Chen Ko Hua

目錄 Contents

1   丑神——觀馬歇·馬叟
     Clown Spirit— Watching Marcel Marceau 2

2   今生 This Life 6

3   此刻沒有嬰兒誕生
     No Children Are Being Born in This Instant 8

4   無眼界 Vision Minus Eyes...12

5   無明之淚 unbright tears..14

6   寂寞·Autopsy Loneliness·Autopsy.................................16

7   鋨實驗 Experiment with Osmium 20

8   臺灣風景——寫給二十一世紀的陳映真
     Taiwan Tableau— To the 21st Century Chen Yingzhen.....22

9   展開 The Unfolding...28

10   我與我的納西色斯 Me and My Narcissus 30

11   南京街誌異 Strange Tales of Nanjing Street.......................34

12   無 Nothing 36

丑神
——觀馬歇·馬叟

漸漸地，我不再以為
他是以他的哀傷取悅我了——
在擁擠着象徵與暗示的舞臺
因為想像的微風
拂動了，輕輕觸響了幾個內心的音節
而顯得遼闊

他說他孤獨。

他寫詩。更不着痕跡的，
他玩弄着柔軟的符號——
他綑綁他自己
他雕鏤着時間
他與自己拔河——可憐的孩子，
彷彿因為太多的試探
而變得寂寞，唉，而認真地在一旁
玩着只有自己懂得的遊戲。
然後他被撕扯
許多看得見的精靈正爭着要他，
他被自己的影子絆倒了
他打破房間所有的鏡子
他想逃離：
他執我的手，教我撫摸——

逃不走了……，我同意着，
許多沉默的理念
在瞬間閃逝，舞台上
人類正尋求一道生活的缺口
他堅持不以語言指示
他獨立搬動一塊隱形的巨石——

當他滾着天真的皮球走過
他告訴我這便是我們居住的地球
他厭倦了奧林匹亞的工作，他說
他想當個人類，休息一陣子

(1983.10)

Clown Spirit
— Watching Marcel Marceau

little by little I no longer believe that
he's trying to please me with his sadness—
the stage crowded with symbols and allusions
seems immense because the swirling breeze
of the imagination gently voices
syllables in the brain

he says he's lonely.

he writes poetry, juggling with soft signs
that leave less of a trace than words...
he ties himself up
he is carving time
he plays a game of tug of war with himself—poor child,
it seems as if too much probing
has made him a loner, off on his own and
immersed in a game he alone understands.
then he's ripped to shreds
fought over by hordes of visible spirits
he is tripped up by his own shadow
he smashes every mirror in the room
he tries to escape:
he takes me by the hand, teaching me how to caress—

there's no escape... I agree
numerous silent thoughts
flash by in an instant, onstage
humanity is everywhere looking for a loophole in life
he insists on not pointing it out with language
he shifts a hidden boulder on his own—

dribbling an innocent ball
he tells me this is the planet we live on
weary of Olympian tasks, he says he wants to take a break
and join the rest of humanity

(1983.10)

(Translated by Simon Patton)

今生

我清楚看見你由前生向我走近
走入我的來世
再走入來世的來世

可是我只有現在。每當我
無夢地醒來
便擔心要永久地錯過
錯過你，呵——

我想走回到錯誤發生的那一瞬
將畫面停格
讓時間靜止：
你永遠是起身離去的姿勢。
我永遠伸手向你。

(1985)

This Life

I see you so clearly walking towards me from a previous
    life
into my future
and into my future's future

but the present is all I have. each time I wake
from dreamless sleep
I worry I've missed my chance
my chance and you with it—

how I want to go back to that second of error
freeze-frame the image
and make time stop:
you forever getting up to go
and me forever holding out my arms.

(1985)

(Translated by Simon Patton)

此刻沒有嬰兒誕生

此刻沒有嬰兒誕生。
廣袤的寂靜裏，久久孵化不出任何一點奧祕來——
空心的蟲卵凌亂陳列
畸型的殘肢垂掛，
我可以聽到臍帶們在黑暗中紛紛攢動
斷裂，脫落。

此刻沒有慾望誕生。
我一直保持如此清醒，以極度緊張
的清醒折磨肉體，如相鄰的兩顆內臟
肥厚地彼此日夜磨損

因此我鬆弛的小腹嘎嘎作響隱隱作痛
右手與左手齟齬
狼嗥於瞳孔藏匿，愛
則密縫於胸肌。此刻
沒有任何美感誕生，整個世紀的衰頹
盛貯於我兩隻眼袋

此刻沒有聲音誕生。
說過話的
都已在收拾行李——
一種莫明的催促已經逼臨
這微弱而已無力搏動的世界，我必須為這緘默
為這天地難得的噤聲

而喜極而泣嗎？
（我原無須喜極而泣）

所以此刻沒有嬰兒誕生。
絕望如厚厚的柏油舖陳
地球完全平坦
喘息在距離枕頭很遠
很遠的地方逐漸止息，夜黑如磚
堅固地圍堵並守衛既成形的一切
所有答案自己填寫
此刻沒有問題。

此刻，沒有任何問題誕生。

(1985)

No Children Are Being Born in This Instant

no children are being born in this instant.
for so long in the infinite stillness not a single mystery has
    hatched—
deformed, remnant limbs droop from
a disorderly arrangement of vacant insect eggs.
I hear umbilical cords gather in darkness:
a snapping in two and falling.

no desires are born in this instant.
I remain wide awake, torturing the flesh with
an extreme, wakeful tension like two adjacent organs
fleshily wearing away at each other day and night

and making my slack belly groan with obscure pain
right hand uncoordinates with left
wolf-cries hide in my pupils, love
is sewn tightly into the muscles of my chest. no feelings
    of beauty
are born in this instant, the degeneration of an entire century
collects in the bags under my eyes

no voices are born in this instant.
those who once spoke
are packing up to leave—
an inexplicable urgency closes in

I keep my mouth shut for this weakened, feebly pulsing
    world
should I burst out crying with tears of joy
for a silence so rare in the universe?
(I had no need for such tears, once)

and so there are no children being born in this instant.
despair is like the elaboration of a thick layer of asphalt
the earth completely smooth
heavy breathing comes to a gradual halt
in a place far from the pillow, the brick-dark night
soldily restricting and defending everything formed
all the answers fill themselves in
there are no questions in this instant.

no questions are born in this instant

(1985)

(Translated by Simon Patton)

無眼界

來，關掉我的雙眼
用鼻息感知色彩

再關掉鼻息
用嘴唇吮嚐氣味

再封死雙唇用耳朵聆聽食物
呵呵再塞住雙耳用身體享受音樂

再丟棄，一再再丟棄身體
只存意念來想像炎寒飢渴，愛憎貪癡

然後我只需再脫掉意識
不再找尋衣服與容器，便流動了

原來時間如水，空間亦如水
在我如水的存在中相互洄漩着波濤與浪花

是詩讓浪花凝止
我想注視，這片刻的不動

注視罷……，我其實想說的
是甚麼我也沒看見哪……

(1997)

Vision Minus Eyes

here I go, switching off my eyes
to see colours with my nose

then I switch off my nose
and taste scents with my lips

then I seal my lips and listen with my ears to the edible
o then I stop up my ears to enjoy music with my touch

and then I get rid of the body, get rid of it over and over again
leaving the mind to imagine heat cold hunger thirst, love
      hate greed stupidity

after that, all I need do is strip away consciousness
and seek no more after clothing and containers, and then
      flow

and so time and space turn out to be fluid
and in my water-like existence I churn up waves and foam
      with them

it's poetry that congeals the foam
I would like to focus on the immobility of this instant—

but having focused... what I really want to say is
I didn't see a thing...

(1997)

(Translated by Simon Patton)

無明之淚

活着　忽而有淚
像與夢有約　但夢終究缺席
我可以遺忘那夢　但失落仍在
我懷抱這失落　於人間求其次
再其次其次其次　其次——活着
就忽而有淚　但忘了淚的理由
像隱隱明白生　生的局限與徒然
又毫不明白生　身在此生的茫然與盲點
只是忽而有淚　人間之淚
落在夢的夜空　比黑暗更虛無
比星光更
迫切

unbright tears

alive   and suddenly with tears
as though I had a date with a dream   but the dream didn't
    show
I can forget that dream   but its loss still
    remains
I embrace this loss   in the human world
    seeking the next
and the next the next the next   the next—
    alive
so, suddenly with tears   but their cause
    forgotten
as though faintly understanding life life's boundaries and
    futility
then understanding not at all   body in this
    life's vastness and blind spots
just suddenly with tears   tears of the human
    world
falling in the dream's night sky   more empty than
    darkness
than starlight more
urgent

(Translated by Robert F. Voigt Jr.)

寂寞・Autopsy

甚麼叫做寂寞呢？每晚
我都要執刀進行一場自剖
我推測，在人體某處
必定有隱蔽的病灶尚不為人知

斗室裏我看見，一具僵硬的軀體
橫在凌亂的舖上，唾液和嘔出的食物
穢物皆灑在不潔的被單上。
剪斷肋骨，開口直劃下鼠蹊
發現內臟還排列整齊
泛着蠟樣的澤光——我以指尖試探
果然，它們早已冰冷、硬化。

應該是一種腺體吧，週期地
爆發這種難忍的生理現象
在血液，或稠綠的膽汁中
我發現整個體腔都浸潤着一種陌生的
微量的激素，我抽取出來
濃縮，再注入天竺鼠的靜脈
觀察

（甚麼叫做寂寞呢？）

而那些嚙齒類的小型動物竟也知道了
一一地死去。我記錄着：
在那狹窄擁擠的籠裏

他們彼此踐踏而行；他們看不見
卻一逕戀棧着屍首

於是我也得到結論。當我
重新縫合傷口，將內臟歸位
窗外正是黎明，眾鳥喧噪在林子裏，
牆角的實驗八哥兒也起了不安的應合
在箱籠裏激烈地飛撞

「寂寞嗎？」我餵牠
拿我的臟腑

Loneliness · Autopsy

What is this loneliness? Each night
I raise my knife to perform a self-dissection
figuring that in some corner of the body
must hide the secret locus of infection

In the small room, a rigid corpse
flat upon the disordered bed, saliva and vomited
    foodstuffs,
filth all spilling on an unclean bedsheet.
Slicing through the ribs, opening fine lines inward
I find the organs still in good order
but lacking a waxy luster—I probe with my fingertips
and as expected find they have long since frozen,
    hardened.

It must be glandular, what with these intolerable
periodic eruptions, physiological phenomena
in the blood, or in the thick green bile
I discover that the whole body cavity is infused with an
    unfamiliar
trace hormone, so I draw it out
and concentrate it, pour it into the guinea pigs' veins
for observation.

(What is this loneliness?)

In the end those small rodents begin to know
and die one by one. I mark down:
In that narrow, crowded cage
they trampled upon one another; they could not see
and were reluctant to surrender their corpses,

And so I reach a conclusion. When I
suture up the wounds, return the organs,
daybreak outside the window, crowd of birds chattering in
    the trees,
in the corner of the lab the myna bird raises an anxious
    echo,
fiercely beating itself against the bars of its cage.

"Are you lonely?" I go to feed him,
offering up my entrails.

(Translated by Robert F. Voigt Jr.)

鋨實驗

悄悄我在你體內置入一顆發光的
鋨元素。當相衝突的
兩道血流正你邏輯迂迴的軟體裏
初次遭遇，額頭陷入了長考
鼻子觀測心靈
有一座迷你的星系圍繞思想的鉛筆，
終夜打轉，啊是否
遽然發光的左右大腦半球
暗示着地球本質的從此撕裂──
當毒癮發作的知識分子丕於選擇一道潮流
跳入，幽浮撞毀在十字路口
旅鼠於城市廣場聚集
午後的祭神儀式裏
精液驟下如雨──
這世紀末最大規模的祈雨呵
心靈交會的電流紊亂
我看見，悄悄拔下插頭的人世
漸漸沒入一種看不見的黑暗裏
空洞的建築只有
衰竭的心音廻盪其中，我也不問
你胸中是否有愛──
只有那顆鋨元素 讓我輕易
再遠隔着一百場核爆與酸雨
之後
將你的屍骸
輕易辨識。

(1987.12.29)

Experiment with Osmium

without you knowing it, I placed a particle of shining osmium
inside your body. when those two antagonistic blood-flows
first collided in the convoluted logic
of your soft body, your brow plunged into long examination,
your nose scutinized your soul,
and a mini mesmerizing galaxy orbited thought's pencil,
turning all night long. did the sudden shine
of the left and right hemispheres of your brain
hint at a split from this point on in the nature of the world-
    sphere, Earth?
...when, in his cravings, the drug-addled intellectual is
    anxious to choose a trend
into which to throw himself, a UFO crashes and blows up at
    the cross-roads;
lemmings gather in the city square;
during the afternoon sacrifice
it suddenly rains semen—
the largest prayer for rain at the end of the twentieth century;
the electric currents of converging souls are in chaos
I see how this world that pulled the plug without anyone noticing
gradually sinks into invisible darkness.
the only thing left in the empty buildings
is the echo of failing heart beats. I do not ask
whether love resides in your chest—
only that grain of osmium   which will make it easy,
when we are separated by a hundred nuclear explosions
    and showers of acid rain,
easy for me to identify
your dead body.

(1987.12.29)

(Translated by Simon Patton)

臺灣風景——寫給二十一世紀的陳映真

很久了，誠然我們都已墮落。如此清醒而健康地
富裕而理直
氣壯地墮落，（在你眼中）
苟活，或者賴活着
在資本主義的膏粱裏如群蟻
忙碌，而深陷

而且沾沾自喜
像從第三世界來的妓女
攜帶着大量教養和信用卡
流利的英語時髦的辭彙
和建國的法西斯美夢
「……待人民先吃飽了，也就自然而然懂得尊嚴，」
並已儲夠了足夠的憶苦思甜的仇恨
獠燒起遮蔽歷史天空的國族想像的煙瘴……

是的，我們已經衣食足而
知他媽的殖民禮儀
但不包括那些曾經為信仰而擲的頭顱而流的血淚
廿一世紀的我們
比較相信精液淫水和肉毒桿菌素
本土鄉土混凝土三土合一的終極偉大論述……
（喔是的論述，今天新上市最搶手最高人氣商品是論述）

而蔡千惠與趙南棟曾經是我們的鄰居
但我們只用一貫對待鄰居的冷眼與淡漠
在電梯裏敵意地打量或虛偽地友善着
不我們根本就只是遺忘
這塊土壤裏（或是同心圓外外外的地球某處）

曾經誕生的理想與行動
而只顧傳送着卑鄙者的通行口令：
我愛臺灣我愛臺灣愛愛愛永遠愛不完（或愛不夠）的臺灣

是的，我們誠然已墮落得太久
久得像已然荷包滿滿的妓女
在報紙上公開招收更多妓女
「……靈魂的救贖是一件華美昂貴
但可以打折後分期付款的事業……」而
今天的早報那一再強暴妓女的員警再度否認他的罪行
員警手握著武器
面目和政客一般清秀、和藹、無辜

而我們苟活者與賴活者
只能擔心記者又將要來問話：
「請問你們在被強暴時感覺快樂嗎？」

我們的回答令人安心地
逐漸、逐漸、逐漸
變成

是。

（2004.9.18 於雲門舞集「陳映真‧風景」首演後）

Taiwan Tableau— To the 21st Century Chen Yingzhen

For a long time now we've been rotting away. Lucid,
    vigorously
Rich and righteous
Magnificently decadent (in your eyes)
Living without living, or without honor
Living off the fat of capitalism like a colony of ants
Crawling and sinking in the muck

Oh but we're so pleased with ourselves
Like Third-World hookers
Flashing credit cards and fancy educations
Trendy English turns of phrase
And fascistic pipe-dreams of nationhood:
 "...Give the people enough to eat and dignity will be theirs"
We've stocked up on enough tales of past miseries and
    present delights to fuel
    nationalistic fantasies
Blazing up to fill the skies of history with toxic clouds...

Oh, yes, we've food and shelter enough
And have acquired the manners of our accursed colonizers
Those of us who didn't spill their blood or lose their heads
    for the cause
We, in the 21st Century
Place our faith in steamy sex and botox

Nativist Homeland Home-builders Three Lands United the
ultimate grand rationale...
(So that's the ticket, today's brand-new hot commodity is
"rationales")

And Cai Qianhui and Zhao Nandong used to be our neighbors
But we treated them with the narrowed eyes and aloofness
we routinely
reserve for neighbors
Sizing them up in the elevator or feigning kindness
No, we'd simply forgotten
That this soil (or some other point on the globe, way, way
beyond our ken)
Had given birth to ideals and actions
But our minds were on the crass slogans everyone was
mouthing:
I love Taiwan I love Taiwan I love it love it love it forever
and ever (or never
enough) my beloved Taiwan

Yes, we really have been rotting away too too long
Like a hooker with a full purse
Recruiting new girls with newspaper ads
"...Spiritual salvation is a fine though costly
Enterprise, but you can buy it at a discount on installment"

and
In this morning's paper the serial rapist cop who preyed
    on prostitutes
    once again denies his crime
He was holding a gun
He has the smooth face of a politician, genial and blameless

And we live without honor, out in the open
Fearful only that some reporter will come around asking
    questions
"How did you feel when you were being raped—did you
    enjoy it?"

Our answer will be a comfort to others
As it slowly, slowly, but ever so surely
Turns to

Yes.

*(Written September 18, 2004, after the premier of Cloud Gate Dance
Theater's "A Chen Yingzhen Tableau".)*

*(Translator's note: Cai Qianhui and Zhao Nandong are characters in a
story by Chen Yingzhen, entitled "Zhao Nandong". The title character
was born in a prison.)*

(Translated by Andrea Lingenfelter)

展開

河流終於遇見了平原
化身一隻多情邀約的慵懶腕臂

白雲終於遇見了晴空
空氣如嬰兒的肺葉開始擴張透明透明擴張成卵形宇宙

眼睛終於遇見了海洋
激動淚水衝撞出眼眶直奔久睽的藍色廣袤。

風遇見了靜寂。
陽光遇見了下午。

一顆拋擲而過的石子躺在湖底。
湖面蜻蜓踩過。

我一人走在風景裏。
逐步展開的風景裏空無一人。

空無一人裏風景逐步展開。
然後我終於遇見你。

The Unfolding

The river finally meets the plains
Becoming an affectionate, inviting, and indolent arm

The white clouds finally meet clear skies
The air, like an infant's lungs, begins to expand in clarity
   In clarity to expand into the egg-shaped universe

Eyes finally meet the sea
Tears of excitement burst from eyes and rush toward the
      long-missed blue expanse.

Wind meets a calm.
Sunlight meets the afternoon.

A skipped stone lies on the bottom of a lake.
A dragonfly steps on the lake.

I alone walk in the landscape.
In this gradually unfolding landscape there is no one.

The landscape with no one in it gradually unfolds.
Then, finally, I meet you.

(Translated by John Balcom)

我與我的納西色斯

最近，
逐漸體力不繼。我發覺不能夠
再只用我這一對枯乾下垂
塌陷的乳房
撫育自己。

「今天該理髮了罷？」我問。
一種對美的質疑
徒然暴長，如一株造型凶惡的盆景

久久我與鏡子對峙
蓄起的鬢角釘掛在牆上，偶而
可以窺見一種命運的小丑臉譜
正偷偷對我仔細端詳

「也愛過了罷？」
我說。是的，而且
早就疲倦已極了——我走過去
強吻我自己
在每一面鏡子上留下指紋
和唇印，一如我怪異的簽名

然而我是如此豐富地戀着（你自己看罷）
在相對立的空間裏存活着的
有無數種延伸與歧異

的可能——然而
我只選擇了你這一種

「而且連這選擇都可能是虛妄的。」我想

因為事實上
別無選擇。

Me and My Narcissus

Of late,
my strength has been slowly failing me. I've realized
I can no longer nourish myself
with these wizened, sagging
caved-in breasts alone.

"How about a hair cut today?" I ask
This interrogation of beauty
shoots up suddenly like a viciously-styled bonsai

I stand at length in front of the mirror
the hair on my temples nailed to the wall, occasionally
glimpsing the painted face of Destiny's clown
sizing me up on the sly

"You've been in love, too then?"
I ask. Of course. And wearied of it
long ago, what's more—I walk up
and plant violent kisses on myself,
leaving lip- and fingerprints
on every mirror as my bizarre signature

Yet how richly in love I am (take a look for yourself)
In the spaces on each side of glass, there exists
the possibility of countless extensions and
ambiguities—but I only chose one
and that one was you

"And perhaps even this choice was an illusion," I think to
    myself

because in actual fact
there was no choice at all.

(1985)

(Translated by Simon Patton)

南京街誌異

我看見我降生在這樣一條街子:
因為三千哩外的越戰
而暴發起來的吧兒巷——
花蓮的小姐妹們,旗袍叉開到腰上
是一個個因失戀而美麗起來的蘇絲黃

我看見我降生在一具薄薄的子宮裏
荒瘠的胎盤,退縮的眼珠子
過度鬆弛的陰道,呵呵
走起路來內八字的母親
曾是紅極一時小寡婦——一隻白膚
金髮的精蟲以他年輕的茫然
突破了層層金子打造的貞操帶
定居到她初次戀愛的下腹裏去

於是我看見我體內揉雜着兩種衝突的血液
當南京街不着痕跡地從良
我成為一隻精蟲誤入的見證
那些善良清白的鄰家孩子喊我:

哈囉OK嘰哩咕嘰。
我總是溫柔地回答:
幹你老母駛你老母老雞巴。

(1985)

34

Strange Tales of Nanjing Street

I saw I was born on such a street as this:
Bar Alley suddenly rich
thanks to the Vietnam War hundreds of miles away...
the girls of Hualien, cheongsams slit to the waist,
just so many Suzie Wongs, all the more beautiful for
    having been cheated in love

I saw I was born in a meagre womb
barren placenta, contracted pupils
an over-stretched vagina (nudge nudge)
a mother who walked pigeon-toed
a cute little widow once all the rage... in his youthful ignorance,
a white-skinned blond-haired spermatozoon
broke through one golden chastity belt after another
before lodging in her belly, in love for the very first time

and then I saw two conflicting blood types mixed up in me
when they cleaned up Nanjing Street, leaving no trace of
    what it had been
I became living proof of one spermatozoon's waywardness
those kindhearted, pure-bred children of the
    neighbourhood yell out at me

Hello OK geeleegoogee.
I always answer them sweetly:
Go fuck your mother screw your old mother cock-heads

(1985)

(Translated by Simon Patton)

無

從無的世界醒來
我可能並不知道
我已經死過

蛆在我體內盤成雙螺旋
賦予原子意志
且噬盡生時記憶——

我乃開始另一程的進化
一如我曾行走在生的龐大隊伍裏
如今　我也曾在死
的無法形容
但似曾相識的行列裏
繼續知識之外的航程——

是的
你不能只以生的知識待我
因為你對無　一無所知

是的，無比影子更輕
比概念更硬　比光更離奇
比死　生　更簡易樸素

但我在行列裏感受你的炯炯虛無
你不在的遺憾化成莫名召喚

終於使我再次
與無　錯身而過

懊惱中又化身情慾的嬰兒……

(1997)

Nothing

waking from a world of nothing
it could be that I don't even realize
I'm dead

writhing maggots inside my body twist into a double-helix
endowing atoms with will
and consuming a lifetime's memories—

and so I commence the next phase of evolution
just as I once walked amongst the vast ranks of the living
now   I have walked with the
indescribable
and yet apparently once familiar ranks of the dead
to continue a journey beyond knowledge—

yes indeed
you cannot employ mere knowledge of life with me
because you know nothing at all   about nothing

yes indeed, nothing is lighter than shadow
more intractable than concepts   more intriguing than light
simpler and plainer than death   or life

but there in the ranks I sense your shining non-existence
regret at your absence becomes a baffling summons

which finally allows me to walk right past

nothing *again*   and in the midst of upset
to incarnate once more as an infant of desire...

(1997)

(Translated by Simon Patton)

1961年生於臺灣省花蓮市，山東省汶上縣人。臺北榮民總醫院眼科主治醫師，國立陽明大學眼科副教授。曾獲得文學獎多次，包括中國時報文學獎及聯合報文學獎，出版詩集、散文、小說、影評等逾卅冊，歌詞創作百餘首，並多次展出其繪畫及攝影作品，其詩集英文、德文及日文譯本將於2010年出版。

Born in Hualein, Taiwan in 1961, Chen Ko Hua is a famous and controversial poet and gay writer. He is an ophthalmologist in Taipei Veterans General Hospital and Associate Professor at the National Yang-Ming University, Taipei. He has won several important literature awards of poetry since his teenage years and has published more than thirty books of his poems, short stories and articles in Taiwan. In addition, he is also a visual artist, photographer and a lyric writer. His books of translated poems in German, English and Japanese will be published in 2011.

出版 Publisher
香港中文大學出版社 The Chinese University Press

封面及平面設計 Cover and Graphic Designer
朱德華 Almond Chu

製稿及分色 Art Work and Colour Separation
明星鐳射分色有限公司 Star Laser Graphic Co. Ltd.

印刷 Printer
宏亞印務有限公司 Asia One Printing Ltd.

出版日期 Date of Publication
二零一一年十月 October 2011

國際書號 ISBN
978-962-996-523-5

本書版權為香港中文大學所有，個別詩篇及翻譯的版權則屬個別作者及譯者所有。除獲
本大學書面允許外，不得在任何地區，以任何方式，任何文字翻印、仿製或轉載本書文
字或圖像。
This collection and editorial matters © The Chinese University of Hong Kong, 2011.
Individual poems and translations © Individual contributors
All rights reserved. No part of this book may be reproduced or transmitted by any
means without written permission from the publisher.

香港國際詩歌之夜2011主辦單位
International Poetry Nights in Hong Kong 2011 Organizers

香港中文大學東亞研究中心
Centre for East Asian Studies, The Chinese University of Hong Kong

香港城市大學人文社會科學院
College of Liberal Arts and Social Sciences, City University of Hong Kong

香港科技大學人文社會科學學院
School of Humanities and Social Science,
The Hong Kong University of Science and Technology

香港國際詩歌之夜2011協辦單位
International Poetry Nights in Hong Kong 2011 Co-organizer
木刻文化出版有限公司 MUKE Publishing Limited